Punch Notes

Direct from the Authentic Wing Chun Kung Fu School in Miami, Florida

Robert Arthur Smith

Copyright © 2014 Robert Arthur Smith

Authentic Wing Chun Kung Fu Scholl, LLC

All rights reserved.

ISBN-10: 1500455148
ISBN-13: 978-1500455149

DEDICATION

I dedicate this book to my father Chuck Smith, who taught me, "I may die trying but not quitting." Never give up!!!

My father dedicated his life to helping others, and I will do my best to continue the tradition. He served in the United States Navy and was a Professional Golfer.

Kung Fu and the Martial Arts are a life long journey.

May God Bless You and always keep you safe. I thank God every day for all of my blessings, including the ability to do martial arts, and lead people in a positive direction.

Sincerely,

Robert A. Smith

TABLE OF CONTENTS

INTRODUCTION i

CHAPTERS

1 WHY WE USE FORMS OR KATAS?	1
2 ZERO MOVES EQUAL THE HIGHEST LEVEL	3
3 YOUR ENVIRONMENT IS VERY IMPORTANT	6
4 ALWAYS KEEP A TIGHT FIST	8
5 THE WING CHUN PUNCH	11
6 DO NOT INJURE YOURSELF WHEN TRAINING	13
7 SPORT IS ONE THING, THE STREET IS ANOTHER!	16
8 MAKE SURE YOUR INSTRUCTOR IS HONEST	18
9 THINGS TO CONSIDER WHEN YOU PUNCH	20
10 4 CHARACTERISTICS OF A WING CHUN PUNCH	22
11 ADDITIONAL TOPICS ABOUT THE PUNCH	25
12 THE BEST P0SSIBLE TEACHER FOR YOU IS YOU!	27
13 CLEARING YOUR MIND OF ALL THOUGHTS	29
14 THE NIGHT MY SIFU OVER-FILLED THE TEA CUP	33
15 ADDITIONAL TRAINING	36
16 FINISH WHAT YOU START	39
17 CHOOSE THE ART YOU WILL STUDY WITH CARE	42
18 YOUR LEG IS USUALLY LONGER THAN YOUR ARM	46
19 DO NOT GO KUNG FU CRAZY	52
20 THANK YOU FOR YOUR SUPPORT AND TIME	55

MESSAGE FROM AUTHOR 58

INTRODUCTION

Congratulations on getting a book that is simple and right to the point. This book is for intelligent people that can think above the basic levels, but still keep it simple. This book focuses on quality, not quantity. Please enjoy it for your reading pleasure, and it is very important to be trained in person, by a professional, to learn the skills included in this book. The reading material in this book is for informational purposes only. You must also be checked out by a medical doctor to make sure you are in good health before you start your training. Attempting to do these techniques without proper supervision can lead to unintended consequences, including legal problems, injuries and even death. The author and publisher disclaim any liability from injuries, death, or legal problems, including lawsuits.

PUNCH NOTES

1 WHY WE USE FORMS OR KATAS?

Martial Art forms are taught to students when they join schools, and are necessary to get muscle memory. Just like a hand shake when you greet someone, it must be an instinct. A person may know several forms, but if they cannot deliver a hard, fast, powerful punch, their martial art may not protect them. There are many different methods of punching, but one must remember the shortest distance between two points is a straight line. Others walk the bow, I walk the string, and so should you. A straight punch will be faster than a roundhouse punch, since it is going a shorter distance. You already knew that before reading it here, but do you really understand it and practice the concept. You must develop a fast punch that goes through the target. The power is not only from your arm, it is the internal power you get with time. It is also important that you do not telegraph a punch, meaning to let the person you are going to strike know it is coming. Do not change your posture, facial expressions, or retract your hand before punching to get more distance, for more power.

2 ZERO MOVES EQUAL THE HIGHEST LEVEL!

A person should always try to avoid all fights, and not use their skills to hurt another person. Most fights end up with one person getting injured or killed. You do not want to risk your own life over someone saying something, such as "What are looking at, or do you got some kind of problem?" The highest level of martial skill is to use the least amount of movements, so zero moves is the best. You may also enter the fight and end up hurting or killing the other person. You also loose in this situation, due to legal problems that may arise. Going to jail is not winning. Revenge also exists, and the person you beat up today, may return to get even. They can hurt you later with a weapon, bring more people with them, damage your personal property, or go after your loved ones. I am aware of several fights that ended up with one person winning the fight temporarily, and getting killed in revenge later.

You need to plan ahead in your mind what you will do before a situation arises. Think out different examples, and how you would react. One example could be if you were at a sporting event and had assigned tickets to an exact seat. How would you react if someone came up to you and told you to get out of the seat, saying it was theirs? Many people would respond with a comment telling the person off, which could result in a fight.

You may be in the correct seat, and be

positive of that, but what if you were wrong. Even if it was your seat, you went to see the game, not get arrested or injured. It is not being weak to get up, attempt to talk to the person first. Do this with care, a sucker punch may be on the way. I recommend to leave, go get security or the police, give them your ticket, and tell them the situation. Then they will escort you to your seat, and take care of the situation.

3 YOUR ENVIRONMENT IS VERY IMPORTANT!!!

Many fights are often a direct result of the environment that you are in. I have never been attacked at church, even though it could happen. A bar where many people are drinking is a place where many fights begin. How would you react if a person that has had too much to drink spills their drink on you? You need to realize that you chose an environment where people are often drunk, and careless. Let it go, and move on.

You may be attempting to enter your car or home, and a stranger approaches fast and you feel threatened. It is very important to be aware of your surroundings at all times. Do not feel embarrassed to yell stop or no, at the top of your lungs, as loud as possible. My Kung Fu teacher would often teach how the voice can often stop the person by yelling with strong authority. Should a person continue after you yelled stop and they continue to enter your personal space, it is time to be ready to defend yourself, with no delay. A delay often ends up with you getting hurt, this is why you must train hard and always be ready. Even though the person may be larger and stronger than you, a fast solid punch into the face, and make sure it is the first attack, will get the job done. Remember you must be in fear for your life, or in fear you will receive great bodily harm before you attack someone. It is important that you review all the advice in this book, such as this example with a very good lawyer and the police before it happens. My father told me it is better to be tried in a court of law of six people than to be carried by six when you are in a casket.

4 ALWAYS KEEP A TIGHT FIST!!!

Many injuries due to fights and self defense situations have been the result of not keeping a tight fist. Over the years I have seen many students with operation scars on their hands and wrists, because their fists were not shut tight. They broke their own hands and wrists while hitting someone. Sometimes their fists would hit the other person's fist midair while they were both attempting to hit each other at the same time. Many other cases were people breaking their bones when they punched someone in the head, and had no idea how hard a person's head can be. I have seen many people that have bent fingers that do not even close now due to injuries in fights, overtraining and hitting hard objects. They cannot even make a fist and have developed arthritis or will have it in the future. Once your hand is injured in a situation, you will not be able to use it to protect yourself at that time, and this often leads to other injuries.

The proper way to make a tight fist is to first roll up your fingers starting with your smallest finger, and go in order until all fingers are rolled up tight as possible. Then place your thumb over them as far as it will go, and squeeze your entire fist tight as possible. Now open your hand and you should notice the palm is pale in color, and then the blood will return to it, and it goes back to normal color. The thumb wraps over the other fingers and stays back, behind the rolled up fingers, so it is not in front. Never allow your thumb to be in front of the fist, thus prevent it from hitting first. I also recommend that you keep your wrist straight in alignment with your arm, do not allow it to twist when punching.

5 THE WING CHUN PUNCH

Punch straight out from your centerline is very important. Wing Chun starts out in a sun character punch, the wrist is bent and the back hand is a few inches out from your chest. The punch straightens out upon impact, which gives it the power above a regular punch. The front hand replaces the back hand, two knuckles above the hand that is now in the front. When punching, the front hand and arm pull down, to clear the pathway of the back hand that will be your punch. You can also strike with the front hand first, this requires a lot of practice to get strength since it is traveling a shorter distance.

Different martial arts teach different methods of what knuckles should hit first. Karate often teachers to use the top two largest knuckles since they are larger. Wing Chun Kung Fu teaches to use the bottom three knuckles. Both work when punching someone.

6 DO NOT INJURE YOURSELF WHEN TRAINING!

Some martial arts break boards, and slowly work toward thicker boards, and many students have permanent injuries since they did not make proper fists. Arthritis is very real, and young people that fight often, and hit hard objects to not realize the damage they are causing themselves. Wall bags supported by concrete walls also cause many injuries and broken hands. Soft cushioned punch mitts held by another class mate is a better method of practicing your punches, and allows the mitt to move back as it is hit. This will not result in so much damage to your fist, if it is tight.

Students of martial arts should also use care not to lock out their elbow when striking. The punch actually will lose power when the elbow is locked out, and it allows your opponent to easily brake your arm. Keeping the punch arm back a few inches will often save it from being broken. You need to move in with your footwork to get close enough to hit someone, do not try to make up the distance by locking out your arm. Maximum penetration of a punch can be obtained from moving in with your feet, and not locking out the arm. Wing Chun Kung Fu has the one inch punch that can inflict a lot of injury, and it has been proven for hundreds of years. A well trained martial artist can even do a zero inch punch, using internal energy, and make a person fly backwards, using it as a friendly punch. They can also make that same punch cause serious injury, and break bones as well. The short punch that is done up close is not only fast since it travels a short distance, but it is very difficult to block. Many people that train martial arts have no ability to block a close in punch, and feel very uncomfortable when someone gets in right in close, and starts a series of fast, hard punches.

7 SPORT IS ONE THING, THE STREET IS ANOTHER!!!

Many martial arts are good for sports, and earning points in competitions, but are not even close to reality in a real street fight. A martial artist that is really trained can make only one punch, and the situation is over. One must know how to do one punch and one kick correctly. This is much better than knowing many types of punches and forms that may not even work. The majority of people doing martial arts do not even have a clue what a real punch is, or how to do it. It can take years to master one punch. Always try to avoid fights, and spending time with friends that might bring you into a fight. I have attended funerals for friends of mine that were attempting to stop a fight, which their own friends were involved in. Two of them were cut by a knife and died, and the fight was not even their own.

8 MAKE SURE YOUR INSTRUCTOR IS HONEST!

There are so many fake instructors only interested in selling belts, and they do not even know how to land a hard punch. Most real Karate and Kung Fu teachers do not even enter competitions, because they do not wear gloves, and would kill someone with one punch. Back in the 1960's there were very few black belts or advanced Kung Fu instructors around, and they were usually about 50 years old. They trained for at least 30 years, and were not making a lot of money running schools. You would be blessed to even be accepted into such a school, and respect was present. I have had many people come through my school and take lessons for only a few months, and then go off and open their own schools. They are complete fakes and have no idea how to land a solid real punch. Anyone can open a school and say lies about their past. This is very upsetting because they are stealing your money. More importantly they are wasting your time, and giving you false hope you can protect yourself. Make sure you do your research on your instructors past.

9 THINGS TO CONSIDER WHEN YOU PUNCH!!

There are many things to think about when you punch, and they must all be practiced so many times that you do not even think about it. Muscles memory and instinct is a must. We have already discussed the importance of making a tight fist, now it is time to consider your posture. Keeping your back straight and standing up right is very important. Keep your knees slightly bent, and one foot a little behind the other. Toe to heel is a good measure, and keep the width of your feet right under your shoulders. You must be able to block kicks with your legs to protect your centerline, block hands with your hands. Some people prefer a stance with one leg right in front of the other which is also good, and helps protect your center line. This stance does not allow you to use much hip power with your punch, but gives better protection. It is best to know both methods, and pick the one you prefer.

10 FOUR CHARACTERISTICS OF A WING CHUN PUNCH!!

First you must have good balance for your punch to be strong. Many people can punch fast, or be very strong, but just like a building, it must have a good foundation. When you punch, your balance needs to be good, and your feet should be stopped at the time of impact. You should not go backwards at all once the punch is delivered. Never back up unless you are taking about a half of step to get out of the way of a very strong, heavy, larger person that is about to knock you down. Then step to the right or left. I have never seen a person back up faster than a person can go forward very far.

The second thing to consider is to have control of both hands of the person you are protecting yourself from. They can be moving in to your hit range, or you could be moving into theirs. Hit range refers to the location where both people involved can not only hit each other, but really hurt each other. Many fighters are not even aware of how close this must be. A long range hit often touches the person, but does not have the impact to cause an injury. Keeping contact of both arms, usually at wrist to wrist as you move in is a good idea common in Wing Chun. This way you can keep control.

The third item to remember and train is to keep control of the centerline. You can have good balance, have control of both hands, and still get punched if you lose the centerline. The same is true on the other side, if you keep the centerline, you will be difficult to stop. Your centerline can be direct from the center of your body, you do not have to punch their centerline even though you might. If you come in at a slight angle, your punch will come from your centerline, but may not hit them in their exact middle of their body.

The forth item to do when protecting yourself is to make sure after items one through three are in place, make sure it is a true martial art move. One example is a true Wing Chun punch. You could also use a palm strike as well, but all four characteristics must be in place that are listed above.

11 ADDITIONAL TOPICS ABOUT THE PUNCH!!

Your fist should remain tight, but you must relax everything behind the wrist when the punch goes out. This will give you the speed that you desire, and is much faster than keeping the muscles in the arm tense. The moment the impact of the punch occurs, you need to completely tighten every muscle in your body. Never look at your own hand when punching, but look at the area you are going to strike. It is best to avoid eye to eye contact with the person you are protecting yourself from. Remember that this information is not for tournament fighting or playing around. I compare it to the power of a gun, and should not be used unless you are in fear for your life. Always know the laws of your state and area where you are. A person that gets hit with this type of power could be killed, suffer a broken neck, or other permanent injury. This is why all fights should be avoided, and this type of punch is used only as a last resort if you think you may be killed yourself. I recommend being an expert with low kicks, so you never have to hit anyone in the face with this type of power. A low kick is hard to stop, and can result in you protecting yourself, without harming or killing someone. A powerful punch to someone's face can be above what is necessary and you could end up in a court room facing time in prison and lawsuits as well. The courts may find you guilty of going over the necessary amount of power that was needed to protect yourself. Responsibility comes with being a true martial artist, the same as carrying and using a gun.

12 THE BEST POSSIBLE TEACHER FOR YOU IS YOU!!!

There are many great instructors of martial arts, and they can show you their skills. You can copy them, and attend classes for years, but the truth is, if you are going to really learn the art, you are your best teacher. You must be sure to listen and pay attention to your instructor, but it is up to you to teach yourself and internalize the art. The next level is to teach other people. To teach is to learn twice. There are many expert martial artists in the world, and they may have mastered their art, and can defend themselves very good. The real master is one that can show it to another person, and allow them to teach themselves, and also master it. I have seen many good martial artists over the years and they can do a martial arts well, but not be able to lead others to learn it. Many of them can defend themselves on an average level. The real master is the one that can not only do it themselves, but make others good as well. I have never met a martial art teacher that can instruct well, and make great students, and not be able to defend themselves. My Sifu said if you want to know how good a teacher is, look at their students.

13 CLEARING YOUR MIND OF ALL THOUGHTS!

My martial art instructions came from various sources over the years. My karate teacher would make the entire class enter the dojo, and kneel down facing the wall side by side our fellow students. We would have to stare at a single pencil mark the size of small pea, right at eye level. No talking was allowed and sometime we would stay that way 10 to 15 minutes, clearing our minds of everything. We were told not to listen to any outside noises, sirens of police cars, which where many in Miami, horns, cars, people etc. etc.

There was no air conditioning so all the windows of the school were open, and we were on the top floor of a building. No one could see in, and we could not see people or traffic as well. He made us clear our minds of all thoughts, worries, concerns, problems, even happy events. He wanted just clear calmness. I remember being very hungry, because you would never dare eat before class, because you would not be able to hold the food down due to such hard work outs, as well as getting hit in the stomach. Back in the 1960's, the Holsum Bread Factory was only a few blocks away from the Karate school in South Miami. The smell of the fresh baking bread could be smelt for over a mile away. We had to even block out the smell of the bread, just clear emptiness in our minds. Once this was achieved, we were then ready to train or fight, depending on the night.

This was hard to do at first, but eventually after several years, your mind would enter a state of complete calmness and clearness, nothing to think about. This included pain as well. Once you achieve this ability, you could immediately put yourself in this mindset where ever you were, and ready to defend yourself with complete concentration. This saved my life one night when I was attacked by three assailants at the same time. They were armed with knives, and they had them out and open. They jumped me behind a building as I walked around the corner, heading toward my car. One person said to me "hey I know you and you owe me money, give it to me now". I also had a knife, but it was in my pocket, and everything went down so fast, that I did not even have a chance to get it out. My mind went right in to the mode of my training, complete calmness, clearness, no fear.

The first attacker came at me and attempted to stab me right in my stomach. I used a Wing Chun block, and the knife never made it to my center, and just the tip of the blade cut my left leg, not penetrating very deep, but enough to cut through my jeans and resulted in a slice that started bleeding fast. You never look at your wounds during the fight, and block the pain in your mind. I also punched at the exact same moment to his face when I did the block, and could feel the crushing of the bones of his face. The second attacker suffered the same punch, and at that point I was aware of the wet feeling of blood going down my leg into my shoe. I knew I could have bled out to unconsciousness, so I ran from the third attacker and cut in front of a car as he started to chase me. I just made it in front of the car going down the road, and got to the other side, and ran for over one mile until I reached my friend's house. My training saved my life that night. What you train is what you become.

14 THE NIGHT MY SIFU OVER FILLED THE TEACUP!!!

One of my first visits to New York was to meet Master Moy Yat, and have a dinner be after class. He knew that I had prior training in other form of martial arts, including Karate and grew up in the streets of Miami. He was also very aware of my height and weight, 6 feet and about 200 pounds.

He sat down in a Chinese restaurant in Chinatown, and the waiter brought over the tea. He quickly grabbed the tea pot, and starting pouring tea into my cup. I already made the first mistake by not getting the tea before him, and pouring his. He filled the cup to the top, and then kept pouring it, overflowing it all over the tablecloth. I was concerned what he was doing, embarrassed, not knowing what the waiter was going to say to me, this was not a comfortable situation to be in. He stopped and asked me if I knew what he was doing, I had no idea. He took another tea cup that was empty and poured the tea from the first full cup into it. He then started to fill the first tea cup again and I immediately thought, here we go again. This time he stopped when he got to the top of the cup and put the tea pot down. He then asked me, what was the difference of what he had just done? I told him what I witnessed, and then he went into a long lecture that I will never forget. He told me that a full tea cup could not hold anymore tea once it was full, so any more added to it would overflow and just be wasted. He explained that this is the same as a student of martial arts that comes with prior knowledge. It could even be a new student to marital arts, with no prior training of any kind of experience that had preconceived ideas of how martial arts worked. He even said a person that comes with a lot of strength and muscles, could think that this would be used as his method to defend himself.

He told me I must empty my mind of all prior ideas and training, do not rely on strength, and do not think about fighting. He said you must learn to play your Kung Fu. A new student to Wing Chun with an empty cup is now able to accept the new instruction, and allow the Kung Fu to enter their mind.

15 ADDITIONAL TRAINING FROM THE PAST IS PRICELESS!!

I was first taught how to fight by my father when I was a young child, he said hit them in the face, and punch like pistons of a motor. Always hit first, do not delay, and do not stop until they drop and do not get back up. He also taught me how to fight on the ground, and wrestle. I also started to learn Karate at the age of eight, and learned many skills that worked, and still do. I wrestled in Junior High School in Miami, and at Florida State University. I practiced Judo, Boxing and anything else I could learn. My point is I will never forget all of that training and still practice it, and would use it to protect myself. I had to empty my cup while I was training my Wing Chun, so I had room in my mind to learn the new skills. I believe that Wing Chun is one of the finest martial arts ever invented, and trust it completely, but I will never forget my prior training, and would call upon it when the situation arises if I need it. I believe that a person trained in many styles of self defense will be better off than someone that only knows one martial art, but you must master one art completely and be able to depend on it. My father taught me about being a jack of all trades and a master of none. I believe Wing Chun properly learned will allow a person to stop and crush all other styles, and that is why I have trained and taught it for so many years. I also believe you should never forget how to use the skills you learned at any point in your life that work, and always be able to use them in coordination with your favorite art.

My father even taught me how to fight underwater as well as on different surfaces, including ice, loose gravel in parking lots, and slippery surfaces. You should consider never attempting to kick on these type of conditions, because your balance on the supporting leg will be jeopardized.

I have also been blessed to train with many Viet Nam Veterans. These brave soldiers have used their arts to keep them alive during actual hand to hand combat, and the skills they learned are second to none. I sincerely believe in learning as much as you can from anyone that has skills that you do not, and spend as much time with them as possible, because the opportunity to be around them, and the time you will have with them is never guaranteed.

16 FINISH WHAT YOU START!

It is very important to finish whatever you start. I have seen countless students over the years start martial art training, and give up and not finish the system. They get bored with it, tired of going to class, and many find out it is a lot of work. Kung Fu basically means hard work of a skillful person, over a long period of time. So many people have such a lack of patience that they get frustrated waiting for a microwave oven to heat up their food. I often refer to people these days as the microwave society. They want everything now and do not want to wait. You see it in careers, money, items, a hobby, and in martial arts. People are in such a rush they do not even enjoy their lives.

   I have always enjoyed Chevrolet Camaros, and have always had one. The one model I really liked was the 1969 Camaro Convertible. The cost to get one was very high, as well as hard to locate. I also wanted to become a better mechanic as a hobby, so I decided to build my own Camaro from the ground up. I did not even have one part, but I had a dream to build my own Camaro and race it. I started going to the junk yard where there were hundreds of crashed cars and trucks, and would bring home one or two parts every day. I would order some parts from hot rod magazines and even got a 6 point harness seat belt out of an old fighter jet that was out of service. I got transmission parts and a 12 bolt rear deferential gearbox out of an old pickup truck. I finished my project Camaro in 18 months. I raced it at the Hollywood Drag Strip in South Florida and won several races!!! I completed my dream and I finished what I started.

One night all my work that I had done was destroyed. Hurricane Andrew was a category 5 hurricane and flattened the carport on top of my Camaro. All I could see was the roll bar sticking out of the rubble, the car was a total loss.

I started thinking back of the journey of the Project Camaro, and realized that 90% of the great times were had when I was building the car. I was disappointed that my car was gone, but realized the journey was the greatest part. This is the same with martial arts, so many people get so concerned with earning a black belt or finishing the system, that they do not even realize the nice time they are going through when they are learning. Make sure you enjoy your martial art as you learn it, and do not be so focused only on the end. You need to finish what you start, but make sure you enjoy the ride.

17 CHOOSE THE ART YOU WILL STUDY WITH CARE!

There are many different styles of martial arts, some take only a few years to learn, others a lifetime. One concern that many people overlook is how long has your martial art school been open, and the outlook for the future. So many schools close due to the fact that running a profitable school is very difficult. There are a lot of people that have been let down, when the school they study at closes down. You may not have finished the system, and there may not be another school that teach the same art available. The preceding chapter discusses to finish what you start, so make sure you do your research before joining a school, so you can finish. There are many similar styles of Karate in the same town, but the instructor you will be depending on may be one of a kind. The instructor's ability and knowledge may not be able to be replaced easily, or at all. Make sure you ask the long term plans of the school and instructor before you begin.

I started teaching Wing Chun in 1978, and for over 35 years, I have been the only Wing Chun teacher in Miami Florida. There have been over 200 various martial art schools opened the area at any given time, but my school was the only Wing Chun School. Recently a few schools opened up and are now advertising on the internet, but they teach it very different than I do. The art has the same name, but the schools are completely different. The reason is due to the person I trained from spent close to 20 years with Grand Master Yip Man. I then spent 24 years with my instructor, not only taking lessons, but being friends with him. The other instructors in the area only studied a very short time with their Wing

Chun instructor, and not even over a continuous period. Some martial art teachers only attend a few seminars and buy books, study DVDs and on line instruction. This causes me great concern since the students learning from these fakes are being taken advantage of, and being treated dishonest. This happens all over the world, so make sure to spend a lot to time to plan that your future is with a good quality teacher, that plans to teach you the entire system.

I have instructed thousands of people over many decades, and several of them have gone on to open their own schools. I have always encouraged them to teach, but make sure they do not change what they learned, and make the commitment to see a student through to the end of the system. All martial art instructors should make sure they plan out their school's future. Once you plan to close down or retire, set aside enough time to finish the last student that you accepted. I also recommend you have a backup instructor, and have a few senior students able to take over your class, in case you have to stop teaching for any reason.

18 YOUR LEG IS USUALLY LONGER THAN A PERSON'S ARM!!

The title of this book is about punches, but remember that your leg can be your best weapon to protect you. The leg is stronger, and longer than your arm, and most likely longer than your opponents arm as well. A well placed kick to the shin will take someone down fast, and keep you protected at the same time. The wooden dummy used in Wing Chun practices this concept in several sections. A low kick is easy to do compared to a high kick, and is much safer to execute. High kicks require a lot practice, and physical ability. They also require more time to train, and stretching is very important. You must stretch often so you do not injure yourself training or actually doing it to protect yourself. My original karate teacher made it very clear, you have no business kicking someone until you can kick in the air first. The first form in Wing Chun does not even include a kick, so that you do not get spoiled to using it, and not pay enough attention to your hands. The kick is introduced in the second form, and should not be done any higher than belt level.

I train in black pants that are regular loose fitting jeans, the same ones I wear everyday throughout my day. I also wear comfortable black tennis shoes in my Kung Fu class, the same ones I wear in the street. Many people wear loose martial art uniforms, and also train barefoot. Then they go about their daily activities wearing shoes and tight fitting pants. The reality is if you have to defend yourself wearing tight pants, you will not be able to even perform the kick you have practiced so many times in class. Your shoes will interfere with your kick since you might be used to kicking with the ball of your bare foot in class. Now you have two major problems, it is like having a firearm with no bullets. I practicing kicking with the heel of my foot, keeping it well supported in a straight line with my leg. There is a saying from the masters in Kung Fu, when you are kicking, the heels must face each other. Both legs must be kept a little bent. The supporting leg that you stand one must be well grounded, and you do not get moved out of the position, or you will lose the power of the kick since it is not supported. The leg that kicks must not be locked out, since it can cause severe injuries to you and will not have the penetrating power you need.

I practice standing on one leg in my first form in Wing Chun Kung Fu, it is known as Golden Rooster. This also prepares you for the second form, where the kicks are introduced. I hold my kick out for at least the count of five, keeping both legs bent a little, the kick leg is at belt level. I would not even kick as high as belt level, but if you can hold it out that high, lower kicks are even easier. I have personally caught opponent's legs high in the air when they attempted to kick me in the face. All you have to do then is lift it straight up as you walk in fast, the punch can then be used to the groin area or just push the person straight down into the ground. That will be the last high kick you see from them. I have my students practice kicking drills, where we practice the exact same kick from the forms and the Jong. The advantage of doing kicking drills is you can practice a few hundred kicks in a row each time you work out. A person that does not do this will only have practiced a few kicks since the forms only do the kicks a few times in each form, and a few times on the entire jong form.

You need to practice kicking on both legs, unless you have a medical condition that prevents you from doing it. Many students practicing kicking out their leg too fast, and locking it out. I have seen many people cause injuries to themselves when training martial art kicks. There is no resistance when kicking in the air, like when you are doing a form. It is better to kick slow and accurate, just like you should train your punch. Many students have asked me how to punch fast, and how to kick fast. The answer is the same, first you must do it slow and accurate, then gradually increase the speed and power.

High level martial artists can see how a person is standing and how much weight is on each leg. Kick the leg that is supporting the most body weight to take a person down. Kicking to the knee will take someone down fast, and it can also cause serious life time problems to the person being kicked. They may need complicated knee surgery and suffer for the rest of their lives. I recommend to do the least harm possible to the person attacking you, but never risk holding back because you may not deliver enough energy to take the person down. You then may end up getting hurt, because you were not giving it your all. This is also known as do not stand on ceremony in Kung Fu. That is why it is so important to avoid all situations that make you use your martial art. It has been repeated in this book, and that is because it is very important to avoid so many problems.

19 DO NOT GO KUNG FU CRAZY!!!

Martial arts are fun to learn, and necessary to protect yourself. There are some people that have only one interest in life, and that is martial arts. I believe a person should be well rounded in many areas, and have several interests. I have been aware of some people that train seven days a week, all year long. My Sifu called this going Kung Fu crazy!!!! I know that you need to practice a lot to be good at martial arts, but do not go overboard and spend all your free time doing it. I enjoy spending time with my family, which is more important than doing Kung Fu. I also enjoy hunting, fishing, racing cars legally, and Kung Fu. I have made so many nice friendships over the years spending time in my Kung Fu classes. We often go out to eat after each class, and spending time together. This is what is known as Kung Fu life. Do not allow yourself to be focused on your martial art only for the purpose of beating someone up or defending yourself. People that have only done martial arts as their only focus in life, often will tell you it is very lonely at the top.

Consider teaching martial arts as a part time career if that interests you. Most people that teach martial arts do not get financially rich doing it, but they keep their own martial art skills up, make a little money, and develop a nice group of friends. Marital art schools that are financially successful usually have to commercialize the art. This can mean, selling belts, uniforms, trophies, competitions and teaching large groups of students, with several instructors. This also involves selling financial agreements and the quality of the school goes down. The original martial art schools of the 1960's and decades to follow, would often have small class sizes. The instructor would barely make enough money just to cover the overhead, but this was often the true martial arts, being passed on the way they were hundreds of years ago. You would be blessed to find such a school, and the teacher was often a quality person interested in you learning the art, more than the dollar bill.

20 THANK YOU FOR YOUR SUPPORT AND TIME!!

Thank you for reading this book, and I hope it will give you guidance and keep you safe. Many of the topics you read were probably things that you were aware of, but to really be mastered, must be repeated over and over again. I have seen so many students over the years that have followed the advice in this book, and kept themselves safe and clear of problems. I have also seen many people ignore the basic facts presented in this book, and it caused them many problems, and even their own lives. I have known people to serve time in prison, lose their families, money, health, and their own lives by ignoring what seems to be such basic, simple information. Please re read this book from time to time, and allow the information to sink in and become instinctive in your life. One of the biggest mistakes that can be made is a delay in a decision, so please study and internalize the topics in this book. May God bless you and always protect you.

PUNCH NOTES

MESSAGE FROM THE AUTHOR

I started training martial arts in 1968.

My father was a Chief Petty Officer in the Navy in the 1940's and was a swimming instructor for Special Forces, which were known as Frogmen, which are like the Navy Seals now. He was an expert fighter and swimmer and started to train me swimming and wrestling as young as 3 years old. I started taking Karate classes in 1968, and also was blessed to live next door to a gentleman in 1971, that that was an expert in Karate. He trained with the Navy Seals, and did undercover work for the United States of America. I continued to take Karate lessons through high school and worked out with friends that trained in various martial arts. I still practice and train Karate on my own, with my original instructor who is almost 70 years old, and I am blessed to be his only student. I do not train anyone Karate, and have dedicated myself to passing Wing Chun on, with no changes, or any of my own ideas. I pass it on exactly how I was taught.

I started Wing Chun Kung Fu in 1977 under Sifu Rex Aperauch, and continued to train with him during my college years. Sifu Aperauch is an expert in Kung Fu and he introduced me to his instructor Master Moy Yat. Yip Man was Moy Yat's instructor and close friend for many years. I was a close student of Sifu Rex Aperauch and Moy Yat for over 24 years.

I also hold several degrees from various Universities including a Bachelor of Science Degree in Business from Florida State University, and a Master's Degree in Education from the University of Miami. I also worked in the Public School System as a Math Teacher for over 25 years. I was in a low income, public school near downtown Miami, teaching teenagers that had many challenges.

I have trained martial arts to several branches of our military, multiple police departments, correction officers and civilians.

Thank you for taking your time to read my book and I hope that you enjoy it. Please contact me for seminars or lessons. I can be located by searching the internet for Robert A. Smith, Wing Chun Kung Fu, in Miami Florida.

Sincerely,

Robert A. Smith

Made in the USA
Lexington, KY
31 July 2014